Truly a serendipitous journey only explained by God's love.

Dr. Marquart

A real and raw miracle story of a tragic event turned into something beautiful because April chose to keep God as the center focal point through it all. I could relate to her pain as she pushed through to find something beautiful. The ending had me gasping aloud and smiling all at the same time. A wonderful reminder that there is always beauty for ashes and how God is GOOD ALL OF THE TIME!

Jessica Prukner
Reader and National Speaker

April's book, Broken Redefined, is an encouraging and inspiring read. You feel God's grace and promise given in the Bible verse Jeremiah 29:11 throughout the book. Broken Redefined takes you on a journey with her. You feel every one of the raw emotions expressed throughout the pages. It is an easy, honest, and compelling read, and I highly recommend its encouragement to all

ᴚdesma
Reader

A very heartfelt and moving story of how God truly works in each of our lives. Wow! God really does answer our prayers! This story inspires me to never give up and to have the confidence our Heavenly Father is always with us. My favorite verse referenced was Matthew 6:34 (NLT), "So don't worry about tomorrow, for tomorrow will bring its own worries. Today's trouble is enough for today. Today's trouble is enough for today."

Shannon Dove
Reader

The author takes us on her journey of healing and forgiveness. She challenges the reader to examine their own disappointments and pain, encouraging healing through faith. This book is well-written and allows the reader to appreciate the strength of vulnerability.

Christina Tipton
Co-Founder of Tipton Ministries

If you're looking for a book about God's love, look no further. April takes you through deep and raw emotions on her journey to healing. April continually felt God's love through the people in her life and the community that surrounded her. He showed her grace every step of the way, as she learned how to fully trust Him through it all.

Melissa Woodard
Friend and Neighbor

April's story, as unbelievable as it sounds, is 100% true. I watched it unfold. When she told me she had it in her heart to write a book, I knew she could and would. She had such a powerful, incredible story to share. April is living God's story of redemption, healing, and love.

Caroline Hogan
Reader

BROKEN
Redefined

A Journey to Physical
& Spiritual Healing

APRIL DELOR

UNITED HOUSE

ISBN: 978-1-952840-06-7

UNITED HOUSE Publishing
Waterford, Michigan
info@unitedhousepublishing.com
www.unitedhousepublishing.com

Author Photo: Tiffani Simpson Photography

Cover and interior design:
Matt Russell, Marketing Image, mrussell@marketing-image.com

Printed in the United States of America
2021—First Edition

SPECIAL SALES
Most UNITED HOUSE books are available at special quantity discounts when purchased in bulk by corporations, organizations, and special-interest groups. For information, please e-mail orders@unitedhousepublishing.com

Some names in this book were changed or left out for privacy.

Julia Cobb
JuCanFoundation.org

*I want to dedicate this book to Julia Cobb, an angel sent
to earth who showed me what the love of Jesus looks like
through the eyes of a child. Her journey to fight cancer
encouraged and saved me during my journey in 2017.
Though she is no longer walking on Earth with us,
she is where my journey with Jesus really began, and
I know she is flying high watching over us. I also want
to thank EVERYONE who helped me in any way
during 2017. Every single one of you was an answer to
prayer during my time of healing. I love all of you
and thank all of you for your love, kindness, and support.*

Contents

Chapter One

*"I know what I'm doing. I have it all planned out --
plans to take care of you, not abandon you, plans
to give you the future you hope for."*
Jeremiah 29:11, MSG

Setting the Stage

JANUARY:

As I approached a curve on a two-lane road, a maroon
car began to enter my lane. Slowly, the car drifted as though
someone had fallen asleep or passed out at the wheel. I only
came to this conclusion because I do not recall any sign of
the driver trying to return to their own lane. Suddenly, the car
accelerated faster and entered deeper into my lane. I had no
place to go. I swerved and all I could do was grip the steering
wheel tightly and brake as hard as I could. It was like watching
a movie. I knew it was going to happen, and I couldn't stop
it. I felt so helpless. The maroon car hit me head-on, and then
it hit me again on the driver side door. The sound of the cars
crashing, the glass breaking, the airbag sucker-punched me,
the smell of the engine burning, and the sound of the horn—
those are details you don't forget.

That day, Wednesday, January 25, 2017, would forever
change my life. Ambulances rushed to the scene along with
the fire department, police cars, and those who witnessed the
event. It felt like a bad dream, but I wasn't sleeping. I wasn't
going to wake up. This was real, and it was scary. I felt terrified
and unsure of what was to come. Initially, I honestly felt as
though I could walk away. There was no pain, and thankfully,

all of my teeth and limbs seemed to be intact. I knew because I checked in the mirror to make sure there was no blood, missing teeth, or cuts. There was smoke coming from the engine, and I was scared it would start on fire. I tried to push my way out of the Jeep, but I realized quickly I wasn't going anywhere. I felt intense, piercing pain in my right ankle and leg as I tried to move towards the door to get out. I began to yell for help as I panicked about the engine. Some pedestrians tried to pry my door off without success, and another one pushed the hood of the Jeep up to disconnect the battery to stop the horn from honking. I gave someone my husband's phone number, and he called him on his phone, but my husband didn't answer. We then searched and found my phone on the floor, and I called him from my number, which he answered. This was a disaster because upon hearing his voice, I became hysterical. All I wanted was this to be a bad dream and for some reassurance I'd be alright. I started making other phone calls to friends to start praying for me and to meet me at the hospital. All of this while the firemen were discussing taking my door off with the jaws of life. It was surreal. We see these things happen on TV, but I never thought it would be me…NEVER! I mean, I'm a good, responsible driver! But true accidents can happen to anyone.

In the back of the ambulance, the young EMT told me he would give me drugs to make me high—legally, of course. He said other things that struck me as crazy at the time, but he had me laughing hysterically, and it helped take my mind off my pain.

My husband and son soon arrived at the hospital followed by my sister Shannon, and my friends Melissa, Marla, Don, and Karen. We prayed for direction and healing. We also prayed for the driver of the car that hit me and the other driver that was hit coming from the opposite direction. My x-rays revealed I had a pilon fracture, a break low on the shin near the ankle. Shannon told me this is a common car accident injury and meant I could lose my leg. Yikes! Because I was pressing the brake pedal so hard, the impact momentum shot up and broke my leg. Yes, it's as gross as it sounds, and it makes me cringe every time I think about it. By looking at my leg at that moment, you'd never know it was broken from the outside. Not to mention, I was not experiencing any pain or signs of whiplash, bruises, scratches, headaches, seatbelt burn, or anything else—just the pain in my broken right leg. That seemed completely crazy and amazing all by itself since I felt like an earthquake had rocked my world. The doctors were amazed I didn't have one single bruise. Not one. It gave me chills as I replayed the accident over and over in my head. How could this be? I was told it was a 100 mile-an-hour impact between the two of us head-on and a second hit on my driver's side door. I crumbled into tears as I understood what this meant. God had His hand of protection on me; it wasn't my time to go, and He had big future plans for me.

The rest of that day was a bit of a blur. They had me on some heavy-duty pain medications. We signed some papers for surgery, and I was knocked out asleep most of the night.

As I reflect back on that day, it brings me to an important conclusion. We often look well put-together and unscathed on the outside, but it doesn't mean we aren't broken on the inside.

Sometimes, we miss it because we can't see it. You couldn't tell how bad my leg was just by looking at it from the outside. We made all sorts of assumptions but didn't know for sure. The doctors needed to examine what was happening on the inside to see how bad it really was. They had to dig deeper than the surface to figure it out. Because they were willing to take the time and patience to get to the root of my pain, they could then come to a conclusion on how to fix it so I could walk again. When we are willing to dig deeper than the surface, we show people we care about them, that they matter. God does the same thing for us. He wants our hearts to be healthy on the inside so we can be ready to receive all He has for us on the outside.

First Surgery

That evening, I had surgery that consisted of placing metal rods in and out of my leg (termed external fixator) and one rod through my heel. This was in preparation to have a future second surgery to put metal in my leg to make the internal swelling go down. Talk about feeling like a freak show. It was scary to look at, so I kept it wrapped up in bandages.

The next morning, one of the doctors came in early and informed me I might be going home. I started to cry hysterically and told him he was crazy! There was no way I could go home and manage this external fixator and risk falling on it, damaging my leg even more. He probably thought I was being neurotic, but it was only the next morning! I was also on a lot of medications, and getting myself into a car wasn't on my agenda yet. My doctor, Dr. Marquart, the orthopedic surgeon, came in and suggested I stay for a few more days or until he felt I was able to go home.

Within the first forty-eight hours, I experienced a rollercoaster of emotions. I was angry this happened to me, and I didn't know why. I was even angrier that nobody could tell me how this happened. I had my own theory, that the man had fallen asleep or passed out behind the wheel. I already knew from the police report he wasn't drunk or on drugs. He was older, so I felt I could rule out texting or talking on the phone. I decided to investigate on my own by calling the police officer who took his statement. The officer repeated the man's words, "I don't remember what happened." Between the police report and those words, I felt like I had no real answers.

In the meantime, we did as we were advised and secured a lawyer to ensure all medical bills would be paid by my car insurance. I went through a couple of days obsessing over why this happened to me. Why God? Why me? What happened to this man to allow his car to hit mine?

As funny as this may sound, God still prompted me to do His work while I lay in that hospital bed. I had a lot of time on my hands lying there, and anger has a way of consuming your days if you allow it. So, I didn't let anger hinder me from sharing God's love by telling strangers about my accident. I made it very clear how God kept me safe. I truly believed He did. I was supposed to go on a mission trip that summer, but I declined to go because I didn't feel led to go. Sometimes our plans don't line up with God's plan.

Let me also make this clear: I don't believe God did this to me. God doesn't make bad things happen. Sometimes bad things happen to good people. My pastor says quite often, "Satan will steal your lunch and leave a sticky note saying God did it."

The thief comes only to steal and kill and destroy; I have
come so they may have life, and have it to the full.
John 10:10, NIV

I firmly believe God protected me in that car that day from any other damage. His word proves He's in the business of restoring, not destroying.

A couple of days later, I was still trying to find the man who caused the accident and learn what had happened. But this task still seemed humanly impossible. I needed to stop being a victim and start acting more like a missionary. *If I'm going to lie in bed all day and talk to people, I might as well be productive about it.* Don't get me wrong, I still had moments of weakness and strong emotions.

I had Bible verses printed out and hung on my wall for me to recite daily. My church family brought them when they came to visit me after the accident. Those pieces of paper and perfectly arranged words kept me grounded and somehow saved me every single day. I never felt love like I did then. I had people in my life I could count on and call on for anything. And believe me, I called on them a lot! Some days, I called several people for several things. Other days, I slept as much as I could as the pain was too much to bear. I had lots of visitors. Even a couple of parents from the daycare where I worked visited me and brought their children. It refreshed my soul to see those little faces. My husband and son came up to the hospital every single day. They hung out in my room, brought me clean clothes, things to do, and the occasional strawberry smoothie from the cafeteria. Those smoothies refreshed me on a daily basis through those tough days. I know it wasn't easy for them to visit, but they did and without complaint.

I'm a firm believer that life is made up of moments which will make you or break you. Not every moment will define you, *but* some moments will add definition to your life. Recognize those moments and build off them.

What moments in life have you let define you?

What moments have added definition to your life?

Take a moment to write them down and reflect on them.

Chapter Two

*Don't look out only for your own interests,
but take an interest in others, too.*

Philippians 2:4, NLT

Roommate

My hospital roommate, Birdie was a fragile-looking elderly woman who'd fallen and broken her back. She had a large family who visited every single day, and they were friendly to me as well. I looked forward to their visits. I'd get to hear family stories as they laughed and joked. We came to know each other by first name, and they even brought me smoothies when they came to visit. Something about that sweet treat brightened my day. Funny thing is, I never mentioned I even liked smoothies; they just gave one to me.

Birdie was spunky and sweet. The way she carried herself and her mannerisms reminded me a lot of my Grandma Reatha. Over those couple of days, I became quite attached to my elderly roommate as she was a sweet reminder of my Grandma, who passed away over fifteen years ago and I miss her dearly. I'd glance at Birdie and even her profile looked the same. She talked and walked like my grandma. She was petite and frail with strawberry blonde and greyish colored hair and her smile was the same as my Grandma's. She was fun to talk to and get to know. She liked to sneak out of bed at night, so she had to wear alarm belts on her arms so the nurses would be alerted if she tried to get out of bed on her own. However, Birdie knew how to take those alarms off and sneak out of bed. She was only caught because she shut the main door for privacy. I hope I'm as brave and spunky as her in my elderly years. I felt somewhat responsible for Birdie since we shared a room, so if she tried to get out of bed, I'd alert the nurses. I didn't want her to fall and injure herself or worse.

Birdie's daughter Marie really appreciated my attentiveness to her and expressed it to me when she visited. Marie would visit my side of the room to talk to me and ask me questions about my leg. I told her my story and expressed God's protection over me on the day of my accident. I really tried to plant those seeds every chance I got.

When the day came for Birdie to go home, Marie came to pick her up, but they had to wait a long time for the release papers. While they were waiting for the paperwork, we chatted, and they both made their way over to my side of the room to say goodbye. Marie hugged me and gave me her phone number. My sweet, frail roommate Birdie leaned down and hugged me.

"You are a tough old bird," I told her, smiling.

"That's what my husband used to call me before he died." It brought tears to my eyes at the sight of her sadness without her husband as she looked down and away from me for a moment. Birdie grabbed my hand, just like my Grandma used to, and stroked it gently with her wrinkled, soft, frail hand. Then, she patted my hand in the same way my Grandma always had. Birdie lifted her hand and rubbed my cheek, and I closed my eyes so I wouldn't forget that moment. I shed a few tears as I imagined my own Grandma's hands touching my cheek. It was as though she was right there with me.

Birdie smiled at me and told me she loved me to the moon. Oddly, but not coincidentally, my husband says that to me all the time. After we exchanged numbers, I noticed her last name was also the same as my Grandma's. God really has a sense of humor sometimes. This was one of those moments God created to give me the comfort of my Grandma, even if it was just for a couple of days. He always knows what we need at the time we need it.

As I laid in that bed hugging my roommate, savoring the goodbye, choking back the ugly tears, I thanked God for letting me know everything was going to be alright. I thanked Him for giving me a kind lady to hug because it felt so good to have this little reminder of my Grandma. It felt good to feel God's love in the frail, little lady's hug and a loving pat on my hand. Birdie looked me right in the eyes with a comforting smile and told me goodbye as she slowly walked away, hunched over, and escorted by her daughter. I sobbed after Birdie left. That was an important moment for me because I realized God gave me a beautiful gift at the exact time I needed it, even when I was unaware of what I needed until I received it.

I miss my Grandma, and I regret not spending more time with her. Growing up, I loved and appreciated how she loved us, but like any other human, I didn't always say it or show it. But for that one moment, I didn't miss the opportunity to take the time and appreciate Birdie's moment of love for me and thank God for the gift of memory.

Reminders

After five days, it was finally time to get out of bed to shower. Yes, five days without showering, and I didn't care. The metal cage of rods was not easy to maneuver, and it was extremely tiring, not to mention the thought of falling on the rods scared me to death. Today was "bath day." Ed, my husband, was visiting, and I felt like it was time to get washed up. He offered to wash my hair in the sink and help me change into clean clothes. As we made our way into the bathroom, I looked in the mirror and was shocked people had seen me this way! Honestly, the pain some days was so bad, I really didn't care how I looked.

The hospital bathroom was cramped. Getting us both in there to get me washed up was a bit humorous, but we did it, and we tackled the task like champs. There's nothing like a little soap and some hair products to make you feel good. My husband was patient and caring. He knew this one seemingly small task would help put a smile on my face. The vow during your wedding ceremony "for better or worse, in sickness and health, 'til death do us part" was displayed right then and there. He took his vows seriously knowing things could've been different five days earlier. He showed me the definition of love and commitment.

The next day, I had a nurse tell me I was her last stop of the day. She said she had to choose which patient she was going to go to, and she chose me. She was nice, polite, and had a comforting presence about her. I knew she loved God in the way she commented on my verses hanging on the wall. She thought it was a positive way to heal. She got me out of bed and into the bathroom. It was painful and a lot of work to get out of bed with a metal cage of rods in my leg. She wanted to help me feel independent by showing me shortcuts to doing the everyday tasks on my own.

She hadn't even started when my friend Caroline came to visit. Little did I know it was to inform me that our friend Tammy unexpectedly lost her husband, and she wanted to tell me in person. She drove all the way to the hospital because she knew how this would affect me, and she didn't want me to find out on social media. If you knew how busy Caroline is you would understand that her taking the time to run up to the hospital to tell me in person was a big deal. As we wept for Tammy and her loss, I was reminded of how grateful I was to still have my husband. My friend suddenly lost her husband and now who would take care of her during a tragedy? Wash her hair? Bathe her when she's unable? Take care of her when she's sick? This seemed so unfair. My heart ached for her, and I felt so helpless in the hospital unable to go anywhere. The people in my life are remarkable. My friend lost her husband and in the same breath, all she could do was think about me and how she was supposed to visit me the same day her husband died.

These are my people, and God reminded me quickly

what friendship and love look like: friends who think of you even when they have something bigger going on, friends who pray with you even when they have somewhere else they need to be, friends who call you to see if you need anything even when their agendas allow no spare time. True friends will go out of their way to make sure your needs are met even when it's inconvenient for them. They will pray with you and for you when you think the situation is hopeless. Your true friends won't give up even when you ask them to. This is how you know your friends are given to you by God. When God gives you good people in life, don't take them for granted. God led me to the right church with people He knew would eventually be my friends. Thankfully, my life plans didn't really pan out the way I wanted them to, but His do, even if we don't always understand at the time. His plan is so much richer and rewarding than mine. Had my life plans turned out the way I wanted, I doubt I'd even belong to a church family. I'd probably not even have a relationship with Jesus.

Later that night came the unexpected move. In the evening, when Ed and Dawson visited, I found out I was being moved downstairs to the Rehab Unit. I had no idea what this really meant. My husband and son moved all my things and wheeled me down to my new room, which was basically the size of a hotel room. It was a private room with a gigantic bathroom! It raised my spirits a little bit. This was the rehabilitation floor, the place where I was going to exercise and face my fears. It was glorious, and I knew God had a hand in all of it. God was on my side. I vowed to make this hospital my mission field. As I laid there that first night, God again reminded me He calls us to do His work everywhere we go, and we don't have to leave the country to do it. We are supposed to be His hands and feet EVERYWHERE we go.

But don't just listen to God's word. You must do what it says. Otherwise, you are only fooling yourselves.
James 1:22, NLT

Obedience isn't always my strong suit, but over the past three years, I have learned obeying God is a lot better than following the path of disobedience. Life can be complicated at times, but the closer you get to God, the less complicated it can be.

Has God ever given you the reminder of a loved one? Who has God given to you to spend more time with?

What friends has God given you that contain the qualities of true friendship? Reflect and thank God for each of them. Consider sending them a message or note today of gratefulness for their friendship.

What mission fields has God called you to and how can you share His love more in the places that you are?

Chapter Three

*For I can do everything through Christ,
who gives me strength.*
Philippians 4:13, NLT

JuCan

FEBRUARY:

They ran a tight ship on the rehabilitation floor. Day one, I was awakened bright and early to take a shower. This was much easier here because the bathroom was huge. Donna, my occupational therapist, was so nice. She showed me tricks so I could do things on my own. We took a long time getting around and talking; then, the next therapist would be waiting for me. This was the routine for each day; my schedule was always filled with appointments.

Alissa, my physical therapist, wheeled me down to the gym to show me around and evaluate what I was capable of doing. In the gym, I saw all types of people with various injuries. It's easy to pass judgment quickly, but I was reminded that everyone's journey is different, and I didn't know any of their stories. My attention was immediately drawn to a man with one leg in a wheelchair. I was struck by how lucky I was to be alive and to still have my leg. My heart ached for those who lost a limb or were permanently in a wheelchair. I thanked God right then for protecting me and keeping me safe as I watched those less fortunate than I learn their new norm. Although these things can be tough to see, I really needed to feel empathy and experience these deep-down feelings.

In physical therapy, I performed various exercises carefully and painfully, but I also met a holistic therapist, Joey. It was refreshing to talk with her. Her happiness and smile relieved the pain I was experiencing. As she massaged my tight muscles, she gave me her necklace to hold, which held essential oils to relax and calm me. Not many people in her position might do this, but she played Christian music as she exercised my legs. It's not often I run into people willing to be bold in their beliefs. I am confident God lined up every single person in my life at exactly the time I needed it. Joey made me forget everything that was going on around me. She really gave me peace. She was the joy I needed, sent by God. She loved God, and this truth radiated from her with everything she did and said.

Joey would also endure my next journey with me. I'm confident there are no coincidences with God, so I'm sure this was all part of His plan. After we exercised, she wheeled me to my next place of therapy. She wheeled me out the hospital door and around the corner where I saw a set of stairs and a maroon car. There I was, face-to-face with my biggest fear: the fear of getting into a car again. The fear that I knowingly had to conquer but wanted to avoid for as long as possible. As she wheeled me closer to the car, the anxiety started to mount and tears started flowing. I felt paralyzed with fear. I knew I had to get into a car again, but I never realized it would be this hard. She wheeled me to the passenger side of the car as I sobbed uncontrollably. I remember her kneeling down next to me, reminding me I was a strong person and she would help me through this. She played some Christian music and reminded me of the story of David and Goliath. She reminded me my God is bigger than the giant I was facing; I could overcome anything with God. Her words were true and I felt comforted by her. After what seemed like an eternity of sitting in the wheelchair, we slowly hoisted me into the passenger side of the car. I felt paralyzed sitting there looking through that windshield. All I could do was replay the accident over and over in my mind. Joey sat and held my hand and hummed to the music. She knew exactly what I needed.

This was just the beginning of a long road ahead of me. My fear seemed bigger than me, and I was terrified. I felt angry that this car accident was robbing me of my strength. I was angry that this car accident could possibly rob me of my independence and dreams. I felt weak and fear paralyzed me. I found myself questioning God. I needed to find strength and hope. But again, a small whisper inside of me reminded me God doesn't make bad things happen, and He was going to see me through this. I have heard more than once that God will bring triumph out of tragedy. He's done it for others…He can do it for me, right?

Joey then got me out of the car and wheeled me back to my room. I told her I knew she was filled with love, and I thanked her for her patience. She told me she reaches people in the hospital often through her faith. I was again reminded of how God lined up all the right people for me.

The floor of the hospital I was on was amazing, especially in the way they ran it. My occupational therapist was fun to be around. She made me laugh and forget my struggles. We talked a lot about everything, and one day, she asked me if I liked to bake. I thought it was a very random question until I remembered they had a kitchen in their rehabilitation room.

Before the accident happened, I had taught myself to bake bread as a means to raise money for my mission trips.

"Yes," I told her. "I do bake bread, but I am no expert as I have only been baking for a few months."

She smiled and with enthusiasm, "Write down the items you will need to make the bread, and I will go buy the ingredients so you can make us some to eat."

"Really?!? You want me to make you bread?"

"Yes!" she nodded and smiled at me with confidence, a confidence in my ability. "The staff here loves to eat, and they will appreciate anything homemade." She handed me her pen and paper, and I wrote my shopping list down. Her heart for me was authentic, and I felt her sincere compassion. Her mission for me was to help me feel capable in a way that felt meaningful. She was fully aware of my feelings, and she knew just what to do and say to help me work through them.

Later in the week, I baked my bread from a wheelchair. It was another one of those moments when I realized how much I took for granted. Baking from a wheelchair wasn't easy or convenient. I got tired very quickly trying to reach and stir things from a sitting position. For it to be easy, everything had to be at the right height and easily accessible. Unfortunately, that wasn't the case and isn't usually the case in the world we live in. My occupational therapist was there to help me with the steps I struggled to accomplish. She never left me alone to figure it out on my own. We laughed and talked, and she helped me to feel in control during a time I felt like I had no control. Nevertheless, the whole staff loved my bread! That recipe made three whole loaves and all but one piece of bread was gone. I assumed they were leaving me a piece to eat since I had baked it.

During the time my bread was baking, I had to go for a pin cleaning. The doctors came and cleaned around the rods in my leg. Talk about anxiety and pain. This was the first time I really examined my leg while unwrapped. The pain from the cleaning was so bad, they gave me morphine. Karl, my day nurse, felt bad for me. He tried to prepare me by getting me some meds before the procedure, but my doctors came in between their surgeries, so I wasn't able to take the medicine in time.

Karl was my day nurse most of the time I was there. He was quiet but had a comforting nature about him. One day, Karl was in my room for a routine visit, and I started sharing with him about the car accident. He never appeared to be a conversationalist, but I was wrong. This led to him sharing about a car accident he had been in. He became a comfort to me during this time. I knew he genuinely cared about how I was feeling, and if I needed anything, he made sure I had it. He was truly a kind man. He talked to me about life and his family. The personal stories he shared with me helped provide healing a little bit at a time. They also helped me feel more grateful. It's a reminder to me that sharing our experiences with other people may help them through something we are unaware of.

We don't always know what other people are battling, but we can share our stories to help others who may be struggling with something deeper than what we see on the surface.

It was Sunday, February 5th, and I had been in the hospital for eleven days, and it was car therapy day again. I had been preparing myself with scripture that entire morning. One person especially came to my mind as I reflected on strong people who endured tough situations, Julia Cobb. I didn't know her personally. However, her story was shared by a friend of mine on Facebook and tugged on my heartstrings. Julia was a little girl who had childhood cancer and lost her battle, but not without the fight of a soldier. She endured pain, several surgeries, chemotherapy, and did it all with faith and a smile. This little girl had the soul and knowledge of an eighty-year-old woman but loved God like the child she was. I followed her journey on Facebook, and she inspired me to live my life differently. Her favorite scripture was Philippians 4:13 (NLT), "For I can do everything through Christ, who gives me strength," which is why I chose this scripture to recite to get into the car that day because she used this verse to fight her battles. *JuCan* was her slogan because of the "Ju" in "Julia" and "can" in the word "cancer." Her daddy would always tell her "*JuCan-UCan-GODCAN.*" This stuck with me throughout my entire stay in the hospital. I knew if that little girl could fight for her life with all the pain she endured, then I could fight to get my life back through all the pain I would endure. She kept me going. I felt her presence around me as I thought of her and the scripture. If you ever need the inspiration to get you through something tough, read her story. She's truly a hero of mine. Even though she's not on earth physically anymore, her spirit is still alive in all the lives she impacted. Isn't it amazing how someone can live on through other people though they have passed away? Her life still serves a purpose through the people who loved her most. Her parents are keeping her legacy alive by continuing the non-profit organization that Julia started herself in 2012 that raises money for childhood cancer and helps families in their fight with the disease. The

Cobb family of six is the most selfless family you'd ever meet or follow on Facebook. Thank you, Cobbs, for continuing to share Julia with the world. She inspired me in ways I could never explain. On this particular day, scripture went with me in her memory when I had to again face one of my biggest fears.

My husband came to the hospital to help me with car therapy. I'd be leaving the hospital in a few days, which meant getting into a real moving car to get me home. My therapist, Donna, and my husband wheeled me down to the therapy area where they helped me to get into the maroon therapy car. I gripped my scripture card tightly as I sat there in the passenger seat crying. I was facing fears I never thought I'd never had to face. *If JuCan-AprilCan-GODCAN*, and I did. It was hard, but it wasn't impossible. As long as I have God, nothing is impossible. I really needed to remember that. It's a lot harder to live it out when you are the one facing the fear. My next step that same day was getting into our moving car and driving around the parking lot. My husband and Donna helped me to slowly get into the car (which sounds a lot easier than it really was). It was so mentally exhausting just sitting in the car knowing it would be moving. This meant for me that the car wheels would touch the yellow lines and other cars would be coming at us from the other direction. How in the world was I going to do this? I had to leave the hospital and go home. I couldn't stay here forever. My husband slowly drove us around the parking lot as I gripped his arm tightly. I held the scripture in my hand and he played calming music, and I sobbed. I'm not going to lie, it was terrifying. Every time I looked out the window, I could see that accident replay itself over and over again. The car crashing into me. I could hear the noise of my car horn blaring. This fear was real, and it was trying to consume me, making me feel vulnerable, and consuming my dreams. This fear wasn't going away overnight. And it didn't. No magic wands, no instant results, nothing. This fear was a process of so many things combined, things I hadn't even realized yet.

I continued to have so many people praying for me daily. A steady stream of prayer warriors continually visited me, praying over my leg. A couple, whom I'd never met in person but submitted prayers previously via text message, came to the hospital and spent time in prayer with me. People I'd never met prayed with me! Isn't it amazing you don't have to know people in person for them to pray for you? It felt as if I had known them my entire life when they showed up to pray. They hugged me, chatted for a couple of hours, and prayed over me. The power of prayer is real and so are the people behind them.

Speaking of prayer, I was praying for the Patriots to win the Super Bowl that night. Lisa, my nurse, rooted, laughed, and joked with me during the game. She brought me late-night snacks. She was my nurse on and off while I was on the rehab floor, and boy did she always have a comforting smile and nature about her I loved. There's just *something* about a person who loves their job. I'll never forget how she dressed head-to-toe, matching her outfit with her shoes. When people love their job, it radiates off them. I miss those that cared for me on the rehab floor.

Not only did the Patriots overcome the largest twenty-five-point deficit in Super Bowl history, but it became the first Super Bowl with overtime. Tom Brady pulled off another Super Bowl win and collected his fifth Super Bowl ring on February 5, 2017. Prayers answered, even during the Super Bowl. I hoped I could be as strong under pressure as the Patriots and keep pushing on, even when I think I'm losing the game. Persistence, determination, and the will to win will pay off. It was the most amazing Super Bowl I had ever watched, and it was also my last night on the rehab floor.

The nurses and the therapists had been so amazing, and they were an important part of my journey!

Surgery Day

February 6th was the day I got metal put in my leg and began healing, the day I became bionic. It sounded cooler and made me appear tougher. The Bionic Woman. As I sat in the hospital bed waiting to go back for surgery, I reflected on the past eleven days. They felt similar to a mission trip for me. You are nervous when you arrive and unsure of what to expect. The doctor's language is unfamiliar to you, as are the people. You start to bond with the people in the hospital as you attempt to communicate about life, family, and God. You hug them, cry with them, and laugh with them as you exchange experiences. Some people leave and never come back. Some stay for the duration of the time you are there. You never know what the food is going to be like or the temperature of your room. You could care less what you look like most of the time; it's irrelevant to the trip. Showering doesn't happen every day. Going into therapy is like going to battle as you face some of your biggest fears. The doctors need to translate their terms to you like it's a foreign language. Some of the people you reach right away, and sometimes, it's a field for planting seeds so someone else can water it. They wake you up early and you go to bed late, exhausted. Most importantly, rule number one, you need to be flexible as your daily schedule may change. They constantly check your bracelet like a passport, and if you lose it, you are in deep trouble. Transportation in a wheelchair can be a little scary at times, and their routes can be long, uncomfortable and bumpy. There's a melting pot of people there from all backgrounds. Getting water can take a while depending on your nurse. People you know are on this journey with you, and you make some new friends along the way. You share your testimony over and over as people ask why you are here. You take selfies, friend each other on Facebook, and exchange phone numbers. Laugh together, cry together, and hug each other goodbye. You take time to journal all that has happened and talk to God daily. Somehow, you knew all along God was working everything out for good. He set it all up. He has a plan for you bigger than you could ever imagine. Whoever said that you need to leave the country to be on a mission trip is wrong. I'm not suggesting breaking your leg in a car accident to go on a mission trip to the hospital, but this just happens to be where I was.

As people who love God, it's our mission to reach people wherever God places us. Our mission field is everywhere we go on a daily basis. We don't just spread the good news ten days out of the year, we do it 365 days out of the year (Matthew 28:19-20). As they got all of the correct paperwork and medications for me, I sat in the surgery prep room reflecting in my journal. Molly, our church prayer warrior, walked in. She had come to pray with me before my surgery. She was a source of comfort, showing up when I needed prayers the most. We began to pray just as my doctor walked into the room. "Can I pray with you?"

Molly's eyes got really big as she smiled and stared at me in disbelief.

"Yes, of course," we answered. The three of us held hands while Molly prayed over the
surgery, the doctors, nurses, and the recovery that was to follow. As we sat in prayer, I could feel a warmth of comfort inside of me knowing God was in control of everything.

After the doctor left, Molly said with excitement and awe, "I've never had a doctor offer to pray before surgery!" Yes! God had perfectly lined up every doctor and every moment just for me.

Unexpectedly, my doctor walked back into my room and asked, "What kind of music would you like me to play in the operating room?" I thought Molly was going to fall off her chair in disbelief of the events that had just occurred. We laughed about it later. Let me tell you, God has a way of letting you know He's got your back.

Waking Up from Surgery

Anesthesia and I don't quite agree with each other. Waking up from surgery takes me longer than the average person, and I also wake up vomiting. Not fun, I know. I woke up in a different room, quite like the first room but with no roommate. I was shocked to look down and see the largest cast I'd ever seen in my life! No exaggeration there. It was bulky, heavy, uncomfortable, and difficult to maneuver. I was unhappy and extremely emotional about that cast. I even asked to talk to my doctor so I could arrange a smaller cast. Yep, that was me, trying to negotiate a smaller cast as if they were going to say, "Okay," and saw it off. This cast probably weighed a thousand pounds (slight exaggeration, of course, but it felt that way anyway). Getting out of bed seemed impossible because the cast was so heavy. I literally cried every time I knew I had to get up to use the bathroom because the struggle of getting up and using the walker was exhausting.

The pain was unbearable. I literally had to time the pain pills to manage to get out of bed. It wasn't always possible to time them correctly, so I would suck it up and just go, saying a prayer for the pain to subside. In those moments, if I have to be honest, my praying sounded more like begging. The pain took over my emotions, and I was begging God to take it away. I had no idea how I was going to manage this every single day, and those thoughts overwhelmed me tremendously.

I remember thinking about how this was the beginning of many new things to face. The next day, I would have to tackle being in our car to go home—pain management at home, getting to the bathroom, sleepless nights, long days, and the list in my brain went on and on. I felt anxious and terrified. It almost felt like when I was seventeen and I gave birth to my little girl Marissa. Just knowing I had to leave the hospital with that baby was terrifying, having no idea what to expect. Just like raising Marissa was a challenge, getting over surgery would prove the same as I literally survived each day for about the first nine years of her life. Matthew says, "So don't worry about tomorrow, for tomorrow will bring its own worries. Today's trouble is enough for today. Each day has enough trouble of its own" (Matthew 6:34, NLT). Today is the only day promised to you, and it's the only day you can live out. Tomorrow is an illusion we all think we are entitled to, yet we know not everyone has made it to "tomorrow." At this point, I knew I had to live today and stop wondering about tomorrow. I had to handle today's pain and obstacles before I could get to tomorrow.

Honestly, I was scared to go home because I had faced so many obstacles already, and I had no idea what to expect. The unexpected was the scary part for me because I like to know what is next. But, in that moment, the metal was in my leg, and I was on my way to a long recovery. I didn't realize at the time what a long recovery truly meant.

The night before going home, I had two visitors. My friend Christina and her daughter Katana visited and brought me a strawberry smoothie from the hospital cafeteria. I really did love those hospital strawberry smoothies! We talked, laughed, and prayed. At this time, my friendship with Christina was still pretty fresh on a personal level. Although we knew each other, we didn't know each other to the core. She helped me through a tough family matter, and our friendship grew from there. She showed me God's love and eventually invited me into her world. Christina always had her daughter Katana with her, and I never understood it. Her daughter was seventeen at the time, and I couldn't understand why her daughter would want to hang out with her mom so often. I guess I didn't understand their relationship because I never experienced this type of relationship with my own mom. Katana, I found out later, loved her mom on the level of a best friend. She did mission work and volunteered with her mom. What a gift to have a teen child who loved their parents on that level. What I wouldn't give to have that type of relationship with either one of my kids, one where they just really want to be with you no matter where you're going or what you're doing. Christina and Katana were truly best friends, and I loved being a part of their lives and experiencing their relationship on a regular basis. It helped me grow my relationship with my daughter. Sadly, Katana entered heaven on November 7, 2017, at eighteen-years-old. This was the year I grew closer to them during my time in recovery. This girl was a beautiful angel who touched more lives than most ninety-year-olds ever will. She lived each day like it was the only day she had. She lived for Jesus and lived in the present. She is greatly missed and definitely not forgotten. I'm so thankful over the short period of time I knew her, I learned so many things about life from her. Sometimes, we need to stop and remember young people do have something to offer us older generations, if nothing more than to slow down and enjoy today, to be in the moment.

Time to Go Home

The day came: Wednesday, February 8th, the day I was released to go home. I slept horribly on my last night as I was in a lot of pain, and unfortunately, it was an early rise day. It kind of sounds like I was in prison. On some levels, it felt as if I was a prisoner to my own fears. A prisoner to my pain. I had to remind myself to stay positive, but honestly, it wasn't easy to do.

The doctors sent me home with several types of medications, pain pills, and aspirin. We took home a wheelchair and a walker as well. As my nurse wheeled me down to the car, all I could think about was the drive home. Getting into a moving car. The yellow lines. The noise of the crash. The pain in my leg. I worked to intercept those thoughts in my mind with thoughts of how God saved me from death and paralysis. A flood of emotions came over me as we approached the car. I felt paralyzed as I sat there in the wheelchair crying out of fear for entering the passenger side of our car, fearing all it would take was another car crossing the yellow line to cause another accident. I remembered and recited, "I can do all things through Christ who strengthens me." My own strength wasn't going to get me into that car. If I kept that verse on my lips, I knew it would help me to overcome obstacles. With a lot of assistance, I got into the car, and we drove away. I recited Philippians 4:13 over and over in my head as I cried all the way home, sometimes with my eyes closed and my hand clenched in my husband's hand. He reassured me the drive was short, and he was going to be careful and slow. He reminded me I would conquer this fear eventually. He played music to calm and relax me. My teenage son, Dawson sat in the back seat quietly as we all drove home. As we approached our house, it was both relieving and scary. Finally, after fourteen days in the hospital, I was home to start my journey of healing in more ways than I could've ever imagined.

Who's strength have you used to get through a tough time in your life?

How can you apply this chapter to your life?

Dr. Marquart and I

Chapter Four

Your body will glow with health,
your very bones will vibrate with life.
Proverbs 3:8, MSG

Homebound

You know those days when you are at work and wish you could be home snuggled in bed all day? Be careful what you wish for. We always think we know what we want until we get it. Believe me. I know.

Once we arrived home, we set up camp in the front living room on the couch closest to the bathroom, kitchen, and front door. The couch was in front of a window so I could see outside and watch it snow. If anything, I was thankful this didn't happen in the summer when I'd be unable to get outside. Summer is my favorite time of the year, with long days and warm nights. At least it didn't bother me that it was winter and cold out, the time of year you don't want to go anywhere anyway.

It was day one at home, and we were trying to figure out a medicine schedule, a careful way to get to the bathroom, setting up everything within my reach, and finding a new home for all the gifts I received in the hospital. The medicine schedule was pretty brutal because I had a two-hour rotation for pain meds. Wow! So Ed, my techie husband, set up an alarm on our phones with the meds to take every two hours so we wouldn't mix them up or forget any. Stressful! I need to note here, I don't like taking pills for anything other than a headache so taking all these pills was not fun for me. Ed slept on the floor next to the couch and helped me with my meds all night. He did this for five nights. We had to focus a light on the medicine bottles every two hours when the alarm went off, and then off to sleep he would go. I had a lot of sleepless nights as I laid awake thinking about what my leg was going to be like, and the pain was unbearable at times. The floor really isn't comfortable, but my husband seemingly slept well. I did learn that he really can sleep anywhere if he is tired enough because I really had nothing else to do besides watch him sleep.

When your husband sleeps on the cold floor to keep watch all night long, that is true love, ladies. He made sure all the right medicines were taken at all the right times. He also isn't much of a cook, but thankfully, my friend Melissa organized a meal train within the church, and we had meals delivered Monday, Wednesday, and Friday every week for two months. My friend Marla, who also ran the daycare where I worked, set up a meal train for a coworker or parent to deliver a meal every Saturday. Those two ladies truly have no idea what a lifted burden that was on our family. My husband was gone eleven hours a day, and for him to have to come home and cook would've been so stressful on top of caring for me and our teenage son. Those delicious delivered meals were huge to us during this time. I will be the first one on a meal train list when needed because I understand the importance of that one act of kindness. We never took them for granted. People used their resources, finances, time, and love to make sure my family was taken care of. Every time someone delivered a meal, they hugged me, asked me how I was, and prayed with me. Without our church family, life would've been harder. So, I say thank you to everyone who delivered meals, hugs, conversation, and prayers to my family during our time of need. Let me make something clear: when you serve a big God who provides for you in big ways, He will always provide the things you need through the hearts and actions of other people.

Ed had taken five days off work to take care of me, but he had to go back to work. I finally told him he needed to sleep in a bed, so he slept in the spare room close to the living room so he could hear me if I needed anything. He did all the housework, laundry, dishes, grocery shopping, and everything in between. My son was on a cruise with his dad and step-mom, so he got to miss the first couple weeks of the crazy life adjustments at home. I was glad he visited me every day for two weeks in the hospital, but he needed to have fun and be a kid.

After the weekend, Ed went back to work, and I was on my own. Before he left every morning at 5:30 a.m., he would make sure I had a few bottles of water next to the couch, and he made me toast and coffee. He helped me with my pills and ice packs. Every morning, I woke up around 4:00 a.m. crying and in pain, rubbing my leg and knee above the cast as he got me the ice pack to help numb my leg. Every time, the pain would heighten thirty minutes before I could take my pain pill. I had to sit, rocking back and forth with an ice pack, crying because the pain was intense. Ed would sit and comfort me. There was nothing more I could do besides wait it out and pray for it to go away. This happened every three and a half hours. It was agonizing. But Ed made sure I had everything I needed before he left for work. The first day he was back to work was hard for me. I remember texting him to let me know he made it to work safely. I was scared he would get into a car accident. I would also text him at the end of his day to tell him I love him and to drive home safely. This went on for a very long time. He understood how it made me feel safe and secure by letting me know. These small actions were all part of my long recovery, and they certainly helped.

Erica

During my first week home, I had an occupational therapist, physical therapist, and nurse visit me regularly. They helped the days go by a little bit faster. Some days when my occupational therapist, Erica, showed up, I was too depressed or emotional to do anything. She would then put all agendas aside, sit and listen to me. I eventually found out she had experienced trauma and pain in two car accidents, which helped her to sympathize and understand what I was going through. She shared with me how she made it through her difficult times. My rough days consisted of therapy sessions of her listening to me, knowing I needed to talk about the accident. She was perfect for her job because sometimes our purpose in life is built off our pain. Her pain helped me through my pain. Our tests in life really are our greatest testimonies. When we share our struggles with other people it helps them to understand they aren't struggling alone and the emotions we feel are normal. The fact we both experienced car accidents and she understood what I was going through was no coincidence. We quickly started a friendship, and I looked forward to her coming over. Each day, she helped me gain independence by getting me from room to room. She made sure I could get to the bathroom on my own and get dressed. She even helped me learn to cook on my own. So, when I expressed to her my husband loved chocolate chip cookies, she brought over a chocolate chip cookie mix so I could make my husband his favorite cookies. It was the small things that helped me feel purposeful and normal again.

That day, when Ed got home, he suggested I should try using the knee scooter to make getting around even easier. We did have one in the shed from when he broke his ankle four years earlier. He insisted I try it. It would help me feel the independence he knew I desired.

The knee scooter was a little intimidating at first because I was afraid of falling off and injuring my leg even worse. The thought terrified me. But between Erica and Ed, they convinced me to use it, and I was glad I did. It made my life easier once I trusted I wasn't going to fall off of it. Even if I would have fallen off, I promise you I had come too far not to get back up.

What testimonies do you have that you can share with someone else to help them through a situation?

Has your purpose in life been built off the pain you've experienced? If so how?

Ed, Dawson and I

Chapter Five

*"Be strong. Take courage. Don't be intimidated. Don't
give them a second thought because God, your God,
is striding ahead of you. He's right there with you.
He won't let you down; he won't leave you."*
Deuteronomy 31:6, MSG

Moments of Weakness

Let me be transparent: there were times I didn't always feel like God loved me in those painful moments. Sometimes my first thought was, *How could you let me feel this much pain when you know I love you?* I found myself calling on people to pray for me because I sometimes felt too angry at God to pray for myself. I know that may sound selfish, but it is how I felt. I encourage you to do the same thing when you feel like you need prayers and aren't feeling like God hears you or if you feel angry at Him. He is a forgiving God, and He hears prayers no matter where they are coming from. Knowing that I had people praying for me added comfort and reassurance that there were people out there who cared about me. Maybe that was the point all along, for me to reach out to others so I could feel comfort from the people around me instead of feeling the pain inside of me. Now, I know God wants us to reach out to Him for all of our needs, but He also knew that I needed to know who I could trust and who really did care enough to pray. Reaching out to others helped me to trust those people and caused me to move closer to them. It also helped me, in the long run, to build my trust in God and to know He was there all along. This process helped me put my relationships into perspective. He knew these were things I was trying to figure out long before the accident. Now was the perfect time for me to call on those I trusted and called friends.

I had scriptures from the hospital taped on my wall at home so they faced me daily. It's how I went to war against the pain. I faced spiritual warfare daily. Then, there were some days I'd call on a friend for prayer. One particular morning was rough, and I called Melissa, my friend from church, who also happens to live in my neighborhood. I needed the comfort of her prayers and friendship badly. I called her crying and in pain. She came right over and prayed with me with so much authority. I was having nightmares that felt evil and dark and with voices that were scratchy and loud. These left me feeling too scared to fall asleep at night. I was emotional and depressed. The amount of medication was making me feel crazy. I felt scattered in my thoughts and completely out of control of my emotions. I truly needed those prayers I received to get through those rough days.

There were days I didn't pray or reach out to anyone, like I was on autopilot and numb to the world around me. There was a day in particular that stands out as difficult. I was ill, dizzy, and sick with a migraine; I literally couldn't function. I called on my friend Lanna to take me to the doctor since I could not drive, and she never even hesitated to take me despite her own busy agenda that day. It's such a helpless feeling when you have to rely on other people to meet your basic needs. She came over and helped me get off the couch and to her car, which was no easy task. I was weak and very dizzy; I thought I'd fall over just trying to wheel myself with the walker to the car. With the symptoms I gave my doctor, he was confident I was suffering from vertigo. My results showed I was severely dehydrated and I had a UTI, and the UTI is what caused me to be dizzy, weak, and sick. Does this not represent the truth though? Sometimes, we avoid doing what's needed because of the pain we may experience in the process of it. I wasn't drinking enough fluids because the pain was too much to bear to just get to the bathroom. I subconsciously dehydrated myself by avoiding necessary hydration. If I had pushed myself to drink more, I wouldn't have experienced the pain or sickness. But here's the thing—I didn't even realize I was doing that to my body. I was totally clueless that I was causing my own pain and discomfort by drinking fewer liquids. Sometimes, we go through our day not even realizing that we didn't pray, give thanks, or tend to the needs of other people. We are so distracted, we deprive ourselves of necessary nutrients: prayer, reading the Word, and doing things for other people. These habits are good medicine for our souls. We, in the end, cause our own pain and suffering by going through life on autopilot. That's what I was doing. I was on autopilot, not giving thought to what I was actually doing to myself until something extreme happened to make me aware of what I needed to do to take care of myself. After twenty-four hours of antibiotics, a lot of praying, and giving thanks, I felt better. When you deprive your body of necessary things, it's going to get sick. Both of my friends prayed with me despite what was on their agendas that day. They took the time to care for me and put me first in their day, and that was good medicine.

I remember one day being in the hospital and feeling angry and uncomfortable. I was frustrated and tired of being in the hospital. My husband showed up for a visit, and he asked me how I was feeling. I lashed out at him, but he told me I was strong and I'd get through this. The problem with being a strong person is you are expected to always be strong. At this one particular moment, I remember feeling I didn't want to be strong and wanted someone else to be strong for me. So I told him, "Stop telling me to be strong. Maybe right now I don't want to be," and I started crying. Sometimes, even strong people need a break. Sometimes, even strong people have a breaking point where pain takes over and you need to work through it. Sometimes being told to be strong is an expectation too hard to live up to. I knew he meant well by saying it. And I knew he probably didn't know what else to say, and so that seemed like the right thing at that moment. But for me, the pressure was too much because I felt like I was being strong, and all I wanted was for someone to take my pain away. I was constantly fighting this mental battle of weakness while trying to stay strong for everyone because I felt like a burden.

Every day that went by while I was home by myself was an internal battle of weak versus strong. I knew it was spiritual warfare. Most days, I'd sleep or watch a movie to take my mind off of the pain and the battle within. Other days, I'd try to read a book, but being on medications made it hard to focus on a task. Most of the time, these distractions worked, but other times, that internal battle would begin. I thank God every day I never gave in to the Devil and his ways to tempt me to fall away from God's promises.

There were many days I felt weak and vulnerable. I can tell you it's not how I'm used to feeling. I generally feel strong and capable. But there's something about being sick or broken that makes me emotional. I'd never broken any major bones, and I'm generally a healthy person. But when I get sick, I am unintentionally emotional. Being weak and at the mercy of others isn't my strong suit. It makes me a complete mess. I'm learning to recognize my emotional side when sickness strikes or things happen out of my control. Letting my emotions rule me is not healthy. Getting emotional isn't going to make me get better or solve the problem any faster, but my emotions are a sign that I am human, and they help me to recognize what's going on with me. God is completely equipped to handle every single emotion we bring to him. David is very emotional in Psalms. Job cries out in anger at God. Most people were desperate for relief when they met Jesus and were probably very emotional when He healed them or when they asked Him for help. Sometimes, in the middle of all the crazy happening around you, riding out the storm and leaning on God is the best way to approach those particular moments. After all, He does tell us, "He will not fail you or abandon you" (Deuteronomy 31:6, NET). I haven't completely arrived, but I'm getting better. I don't know about you, but I found this to be true especially during these moments, and I've only shared a few with you. There were plenty more, but this book would be so long you'd never finish reading it if I wrote about them all. Just remember this, when you surround yourself with the right people, you'll get the right results. Had it not been for my church and making friends there before the accident happened, the outcome would've been a lot different. Everyone needs a circle of people to count on, and I'm glad I found mine. If you don't have a circle of people, I would suggest finding a church first, going to some small groups, and surrounding yourself with like-minded people. Everyone has been through something, so you are not alone. If you are not ready for the church setting yet, open up the Bible and start reading and learning about God's love and all He promises you. God will never ever leave you. He loves you and was beaten and died for you. His words will direct you if you invite Him in and learn to listen to His whispers. If you learn to stay close to God, you won't be abandoned.

List a moment when God came through for you.

Name a few people he put in your path at the time you needed them.

Chapter Six

We plan the way we want to live, but only God makes us able to live it. It Pays to Take Life Seriously.
Proverbs 16:9, MSG

Independence, Sort Of

MARCH:

When I look back at my journal, on March 3 I wrote, "A lot has happened since I journaled a couple of weeks ago..." so I'm going to quickly recap the end of February. My mom was in the hospital, so my sister Shannon picked me up to go visit her a few times. It was great getting out of the house to go on a road trip. Those weekly road trips helped refresh me and get me back in the car. They were somewhat therapeutic for me. I received weekly letters from a friend from my church, and those helped make the time pass. Although I did write back, they were scattered thoughts, and they never made their way to the mailbox. My best friend, Tonya, from Illinois, and her mom visited me, and I had not seen them in eight years. That was the best surprise ever! I cried like a baby. I love her and her mom so much and their visit was good for my soul.

I also returned to my Bible study on Wednesday mornings. My friends from church took turns picking me up and dropping me off every week. That group of ladies sure did help me through some rough days and weeks as I battled with depression, pain, and loneliness. Every single one of them helped me get through a tough time, even if they didn't realize something as small as a ride to class would change my mood from isolated to involved. Even my son who is just a teenager thought about me and called me from school to check on me to make sure I was feeling okay. He even made me lunch to make my day easier. In those seemingly small moments, I realized what a great kid I raised. Those small gestures spoke compassion and opened my eyes to the kind of man he was becoming. He's kind, compassionate, and caring.

I ran out of my pain medications on a Sunday and couldn't get a refill until Monday. So, first thing Monday morning, I called my friend, Melissa. She was unable to go and pick them up for me but her husband would go get them so I wouldn't be without them. He ran that errand for me and said he was happy to do it. There's not a lot of people I know who would take time out of the day to go and pick up medication for anyone other than their own spouse or child. I was again grateful for the kindness of my church family. They continually showed me so much compassion.

My friend Mike, a morning radio show host, called me every other day to check in on me. We'd talk in between his time on air. The small gesture helped the time pass. He made me laugh and I began to look forward to the phone call conversations since I was home all day by myself. Each person's role in my journey was different, yet I needed every single one of them. We take so much for granted each day as we get busy, and we forget about the people who are etched as a part of our crazy life.

I also got my stitches out and a much smaller cast that was manageable and light. I used the knee cart, which made my life easier to get around. I started to feel better and gained more independence as we moved into the month of March.

March was a milestone month for me. I gained more independence by getting around on the knee cart, accomplishing small tasks around the house, and getting outside to get the mail occasionally. Finally, in the third weekend of March, I was put into an air cast and feeling less pain, which allowed for fewer pain meds. I remember waking up one morning and feeling little-to-no pain, so I decided not to take any pain pills until the pain was not manageable. I waited for the pain in anticipation all day thinking I would need them. Thankfully, the pain remained minimal. There was no sense in taking the painkillers if I could manage with Ibuprofen. Little did I know what this really meant.

Almost immediately, I started experiencing withdrawal symptoms, suffering from sleep deprivation, puking, trembling, and mood swings. I felt like a train wreck. I was happy, then sad, then angry, and then crying. I was exhausted, yet my brain wouldn't shut down. It was such a miserable week for me, and I am positive for everyone around me too. There were some moments when I prayed and cried and begged for relief all at once. There were other moments I doubted the prayers were being answered. Sometimes, I felt like the Devil had a hold of me by the throat laughing because I felt so weak and angry. It would've been so easy to take one pain pill to ease the misery and give myself some relief. But I knew if I did, my body would want me to keep feeding it pain pills, and then I'd never get off of them. So, I stood strong and went through the detox process for nine long days. Eventually, my body stopped wanting the pain pills, and all of the sickness and sleep issues got better with time. I could tell I wasn't completely myself yet, as it does take several months to detox completely. Thankfully, my leg pain was gone, physical pain being the hardest thing to control. At this point, life shifted and the mental aspect of recovery became my next challenge.

I occasionally listened to a weekly prayer call, and I remember hearing something that stood out to me at the right time. A great mentor of mine said, "We need to take inventory of what we do have instead of what we don't have."

The book of Mark details the story of Jesus' compassion to feed over 5,000 people (NLT). Mark details the conversation between Jesus and his disciples: "'How much bread do you have?' he [Jesus] asked. 'Go and find out.'

They came back and reported, 'We have five loaves of bread and two fish'" (Mark 6:38, NLT).

The rest of the story, in short, was how God took bread and fish and multiplied it to feed the people, and there were even leftovers for people to take home. God multiplied five loaves of bread and two fish to feed over five thousand people! Anything multiplied by God equals enough. God will take anything we have and make it enough. Wow, is this ever a reminder of God's love! God took my weak moments where I didn't think I had it in me to get through the pain and detox, and He made my small mustard seed of faith enough to get me through those tough times. All you need is faith the size of a mustard seed, and God can use it in big ways. There were times my spirit felt tired and weak, and Satan was attacking me, but God knew my heart, and he used what I had and showed up the way only God can show up. Me (April) multiplied by God equals enough because anything multiplied by God will always be enough. On their own, the disciples could not have fed 5,000 people. But because Jesus multiplied what they already had, and they then had enough for everyone. If you take God out of the equation, then it is us trying to be strong alone. Like a math problem when the equation is wrong, the answer will be incorrect. I realize I am dependent on God to get me through life. I'm reliant on His word. I need to have faith that His word will get me through all things. I'm a very independent person and relying on anyone has always been difficult for me because people in my life have let me down. Giving it all over to God and trusting Him has been a process. I don't know if I'll ever fully arrive, but I sure will give it an honest effort. Being dependent on God and standing on His word is a gamble worth taking. At that point in my life, I had nothing to lose and everything to gain.

What has God shown you about your journey?

In what areas could you work on relying on God?

Chapter Seven

But when he looked down at the waves churning beneath his feet, he lost his nerve and started to sink. He cried, "Master, save me!" Jesus didn't hesitate. He reached down and grabbed his hand. Then he said, "Faint-heart, what got into you?"

Matthew 14:30-31, MSG

Fixing My Focus

APRIL:

My air cast was still on, but I still could not bear any weight on my leg. Still, I was so relieved the hard cast was off because it meant I was closer to walking. I was also scared. I was terrified of my leg. For two months, I had not seen my leg, the damage, or the scars, except during cast changes. One day, my fear became my reality. I had been instructed by my doctor to expose my leg to touch, texture, and to start "loving my leg" again. I am told once a part of your body has been denied attention and love, it begins to die and it won't thrive. My leg being in a hard cast for so long was like covering and denying anything was wrong. It was denying the accident happened. It was out of sight, out of mind. Sometimes, we can't see the scars, but that doesn't mean there's not a battle being fought inside. The cast meant I didn't have to face the emotional part of the accident if I didn't see the results of it. Although the everyday immobility was a reminder, the cast still masked the hidden pain. In life, we sometimes harden our hearts to mask our pain. It's a defense mechanism to appear stronger than we really are on the outside when on the inside we are dying from deprivation. When we limit our exposure to the necessary things that we need in life to thrive, we will begin to die. My leg was no different. It needed love. It needed exposure to exercise to make it strong, a human's touch to soothe it, clothing to protect the skin, a soft blanket to give it comfort, and a washcloth to clean it.

This reminded me of life and relationships. When we deny each other the love and attention we so greatly deserve from each other, relationships and love for each other will not thrive. They start to die, and we don't always notice it or see it. That's true with all relationships. Especially our relationship with Jesus. If we don't have a relationship with Him daily, we are depriving ourselves of all He has to offer us. Things become stagnant and our relationship becomes lethargic when we don't move closer and begin to know each other or Him better. It was almost like I was mad at my leg once I could see it, for failing me during the accident. I know it sounds silly because it wasn't the fault of my leg. It was doing its job and wasn't strong enough to endure that type of pressure. Like people we trust, sometimes they do all they can do and they still fail us. That's why our trust should be in Him and not in people. So, for me to love my leg again when I felt angry wasn't easy. Touching and trusting my leg again to not fail me was emotional and scary, but I did what the doctor instructed because I was hoping eventually the more I did it, the more I would learn to love and trust it again. Every step of recovery for me was an emotional process. Every bit of me was tested. When we do what is best for us even when it's hard, the results are amazing.

That week, I was watching a series on YouTube for my Bible study class, and I heard God speak to me through this series loud and clear. The one-liner I heard was, "Sometimes you can't fix your conditions, but you can fix your focus." That one sentence was so powerful! It changed my perspective, and it made me action-oriented. I knew I couldn't fix what happened to me, but I could fix how I approached it. I had to fix my focus on Jesus and His promises. Peter walked on water because his faith was in Jesus, but the moment he took his focus off Him and focused on the storm, he sank. I could focus on Jesus' promises about healing, or I could focus on the storm. I knew I couldn't change the fact the car accident happened and my leg was broken, but I could change how I was dealing with it. My faith must be in God's promises and not in the storm. I had to remember I am not my circumstances. My focus was not what happened to me but who I am in Christ and what He did for me.

So, I began to touch my leg and learn to love it again. I massaged it and cleaned it. I exposed it to blankets and clothing. The scars were bold and ugly, but I still had my leg and that was what mattered most. In the beginning, I cried through all of it. I cried because I was thankful, and I cried because I needed to feel the love I had for all the things my two legs provided.

These are my battle scars, and they are reminders to me that everyone is going through something, and life on earth is a temporary gift. Those scars were reminders my life was spared because He's not done with me yet. These scars are a reminder of God's love for me when my faith is as small as a mustard seed. These scars remind me every day how God's word is faithful. If He can create the entire universe and construct every tiny cell in my body down to the smallest of details, He could heal my leg.

Every single day, it got easier to touch my leg, to love it again, and to thank God I still had a leg. By loving my leg again, my focus shifted from my temporary circumstances to God's infinite promises for my future. His promises are the same yesterday, today, and tomorrow. They are everlasting and never changing. My body might change and fail me, but His promises won't.

Who or what are you putting your faith in?

Chapter Eight

Jesus replied, "You don't understand now what I am doing but someday you will."

John 13:7, NLT

Pieces to the Puzzle

MAY:

By the end of May, I was finally walking. It was a slow process and my leg was weak, but I had started physical therapy. I never realized how hard physical therapy is. It is both mentally and physically tough. I hadn't trusted anyone to touch or manipulate my leg in so long. The thought of it made me sick. Putting trust in someone you don't even know, who is now your physical therapist, is huge for recovery.

Every time she touched my leg, I held my breath and closed my eyes. The first few times, I begged her to be careful not to break it. I'm sure she thought I was overdramatic, but she played it cool and was compassionate and gentle. She eventually gained my trust, and over time, it wasn't a big deal anymore. Physical therapy was another piece to the puzzle of recovery because it requires you to trust others. It was another opportunity to grow and heal and not feel broken.

Though independence offers a lot of opportunities, there's a lot of opportunity in brokenness too. Once you break something, you have the option to fix it or not. You can use the right substance to permanently fix it or something else to temporarily fix it. If you choose not to take the opportunity to fix it right, there are consequences you must pay. Some examples of consequences could be a lost relationship, a disfigured leg because you were too scared to do physical therapy, or death without resolution. I could have chosen not to do physical therapy because I didn't want to trust the process out of my fear. The outcome for healing incorrectly would have been devastating and would have limited the use of my leg. But, if you choose to fix it, then you must decide what you are going to do to put it back together again. The substance you choose will determine the outcome. The substance can help it or hurt it.

In order for me to receive the best outcome, I needed to choose the substances of trust, determination, prayer, wisdom, and a plan. These were holding me together during the process of becoming whole again. Each day, I focused on healing by the use of these substances, like glue holding a puzzle together so it won't fall apart. Using tape wouldn't hold the puzzle together properly. Glue is the stronger substance a puzzle needs so it won't break, similar to how I needed trust, determination, prayer, wisdom, and a plan to hold me together, so I didn't feel broken anymore. God is all these things and more. He is my stronger substance in my healing.

As humans, we are made up of so many different experiences that hold us together. Sometimes in life, negative experiences or tragedy will break us into millions of pieces, and we begin to fall apart. Every bad experience I had in my life crept in to steal my joy when I was fragile, but when we focus on God, He becomes the glue that holds us together so we can be exactly who He has called us to be. He will bring people into your life who you can lock arms with and who will walk beside you no matter what. He brings hope, salvation, love, meal trains, a husband, children, friends, careers, prayer warriors, and good health, and then this puzzle becomes a beautiful masterpiece we call life in Christ.

I wasn't going to let every bad experience steal my joy. Instead, I replaced the bad thoughts with healthy ones. I consider my leg another piece of the picture puzzle of life. Sometimes being broken is refreshing because it brings us to a place where we get the opportunity to be redefined and transformed into someone new.

What substances are holding you together?

Has life brought you to a place of being redefined?

Chapter Nine

Trust God from the bottom of your heart; don't try to figure out everything on your own. Listen for God's voice in everything you do, everywhere you go; he's the one who will keep you on track.

Proverbs 3:5-6, MSG

Don't Get Caught up in the WHY?

JUNE:

The time finally came, the dreaded day when I was going to have to drive again. My husband was going out of town for two weeks for work, and I would have to drive myself around. Up until then, a car service had been provided for me to get back and forth to my leg-related appointments. I knew the day was going to come, I had just hoped it would be on my timing, not forced timing. I basically had two weeks to get into the car and drive again. I started out my day getting into my Jeep and pulling it in and out of my driveway. I'm pretty sure that to my neighbors, I looked like a lunatic. But honestly, I was terrified of this seemingly small task. I had to learn to trust the brake pedal; I was afraid of the brake pedal breaking my leg again. Putting my foot on that pedal literally made me cry. It brought back all of the fear I had felt since the car accident. I would sit in the driver's seat, the accident replaying itself over and over in the windshield. All I could do was cry and beg God to give me courage. I eventually got to a place where I started to drive around my subdivision. I think I drove slower than most elderly people do. But hey, as long as I could do it, then who cares?

I drove in my subdivision for a few days, and then

I got up enough courage to drive to the store. It was about a block away, across a very fast-moving main road. The quick-moving cars made me nervous at first. When I made it on to the main road, I realized I would have to be next to the yellow center line to turn into the parking lot. I was terrified. I was very hyper-sensitive to any tire that got close to that yellow centerline. I watched every single tire get close as it came towards me.

I did eventually make it to the store, and I was relieved. Who knew grocery shopping could be so much fun after not doing it for almost six months? I was so happy to go to the store and do my own shopping. It was such a huge step to regaining my sense of freedom and overcoming the fear that held me captive. Those couple of weeks consisted of a lot of driving to the grocery store, a clothing store, the gas station, and to fast food places. I was prepared for my husband Ed to go out of town for two weeks for work…or so I thought.

I drove myself to physical therapy for the first time the morning Ed left to work out of state. I pulled up behind a car in the turn lane. She went to turn, another car turned at the same time, and they crashed. Talk about panic. I was gripping hard on the steering wheel as I pulled over. I got out, called 911, and checked to make sure everyone was okay. Everyone was, so I was instructed to leave since it was a very busy intersection. I proceeded to physical therapy while sobbing, remembering the accident and how that could have been me. I was quickly reminded by this small voice it wasn't me. I am alive, still have my leg, and I can still walk. I proceeded to the appointment and walked in still hysterically crying, knowing I was going to have to drive home. My physical therapist calmed me down and proceeded to remind me it wasn't going to happen to me. She offered to call me an Uber, but I understood that would have done me little good. I was still going to have to drive my own car home at some point. I stayed there, calmed down, and decided to drive home. I had to remind myself accidents happen every single day: people get sick and people die, and we cannot control anyone or anything around us. So, I chose to put my hope in the promises of God and what God says my future holds, not what the world says my future holds. I'm thankful God has a plan for me that is far better than any plan I have for myself.

Truth in Therapy

I became lost in my thoughts for weeks, obsessing over, "Why? How did this happen? Did the man who hit me have a medical problem? Did he know and still choose to drive? Is he okay?" and I couldn't let go of it. It was literally ruining my days obsessing over these questions no one could answer. So, who better to ask and expect miraculous answers from than my therapist? I remember going to my appointment with this huge weight on my shoulders, trying to hold back my tears, hoping to get the answers I wanted. But sometimes, you don't get what you want and you have to hear things you don't want to hear. I said to my therapist while choking back tears, "I really just want to know what happened and why he hit me. Did he pass out or fall asleep?" I will never forget how she so compassionately said to me, "Even if you never find out because you may not, will it change what happened? Will it change the fact that you were in an accident?"

As I sat there, tears began to flow, and there was nothing to say but, "No." Even having answers to any of those questions will not change the chain of events that took place that day. Answers won't change the past.

She said, "You are going to have to move on knowing you may never know." Right then and there, the truth kind of hurt, but it was also refreshing to accept. It was time to move on. It would be a miracle at this point if I ever found out. I know this because I tried every human outlet I could to try to get the answers I wanted, and nobody could give them to me. So, I made the decision that day to move on and start the healing process by surrendering my defeated efforts and making the hard choice to give it all over to God. I felt huge weights lifted off my shoulders as I cried and realized that not knowing wasn't the worst thing that had happened during this journey. I had a lot to be thankful for: I still had my leg, I could walk, and most importantly, I was alive.

Sometimes, we lose sight of what's really important when we get fixated on the, "why" Although the "why" is still important, I cannot let the unknown stop me from healing and moving forward. So, I walked out of her office, and I decided that day to move on to the process of internal healing and choosing to forgive the man who hit me. It took time, patience, God, and a lot of self-talk to get to that point; it didn't happen the moment my feet left the therapist's room. But it did happen.

What unknowns do you need to "let go of" and give to God?

Who do you need to forgive so you can live again?
examples

Chapter Ten

Don't you realize that in a race everyone runs, but only one person gets the prize? So run to win! All athletes are disciplined in their training. They do it to win a prize that will fade away, but we do it for an eternal prize. So I run with purpose in every step. I am not just shadow boxing. I discipline my body like an athlete, training it to do what it should. Otherwise, I fear that after preaching to others I myself might be disqualified.

1 Corinthians 9:24-27, NLT

Goals

JUNE-AUGUST:

It was summer, and with the warm weather and my renewed ability to walk, I was able to stay busy and get outside; it was incredibly refreshing. I really wanted to set a goal to run any distance in the Crim Race in Flint that summer. There's no motivation like being told, "You shouldn't count on running this year," to prove to myself and everyone else I was going to at least run a mile. Challenge accepted! I went online and signed up; I was fully paid and fully committed. The mile would happen the last weekend in August, and it was currently June.

I felt two and a half months was enough preparation time from barely walking to running. I mean, it's only a mile; only ten-to-fifteen minutes of my life if I run it. But even if I ended up walking it, I still had to use my legs to walk a whole mile. A mile is still a mile, no matter how long it takes to get there. After all, three years before this, I ran the ten-mile in the Crim Race in one hour and forty-one minutes. I also ran the Michigan Mile in seven minutes and forty-five seconds. I set my bar very high that year because I trained really hard to run a fast one mile. This year, though, I had no goal expectations other than to just finish. Finishing, to me, would be keeping a promise to myself to not stop no matter how hard or painful it might be.

At that point, I knew I just needed a goal to feel motivated. Although the competitive side of me wanted to do it in ten minutes, the realistic side said it didn't really matter. As long as I finished the mile, it would prove to me I could do it.

I added daily training to my physical therapy three times a week. It was mentally and physically exhausting. There were plenty of tears, sweat, and self-talk during that season. There were so many times I wanted to quit everything because jogging was painful. I had so much metal in my leg that when I jogged or ran, I did it with a limp. It was so frustrating. No matter what I did, that limp was still there. I think it was because the metal made my right leg heavier than the left one. The uneven distribution of weight caused a limp and added pain. I told myself that, over time, it would go away when I grew stronger and more consistent. I remember being in physical therapy and struggling with so many obstacles, especially bending and squatting, because of the location of the metal in my leg. I could not get past the idea that I was always going to be limited in what I was going to be able to do. The limitations on a daily basis frustrated me, not to mention, I could feel the metal, and my leg ached every single morning when I woke up.

I made an appointment with my leg doctor to discuss my options. My doctor told me I could get the metal removed because once my leg was healed, the metal really didn't serve any purpose. I asked him what I had to expect after that surgery, and he told me that I would be in a cast for two weeks, and it could take up to five weeks total to recover. In addition, I would be in pain, though not as severe as when I broke my leg, and my pain medications would be mild compared to before. Those thoughts scared me. I definitely didn't want to regress. I didn't want to be on any more pain medications and go through withdrawals again. I didn't want to be laid up in a cast again after just regaining my freedom to walk and have independence. That decision took some time. He told me not to rush into any decisions, to think about it, and that we would talk about it at the next appointment.

Through the summer, I trained and went to physical therapy every single week. My husband was traveling a lot for his job since he had not been able to travel for the past six months. This left me often home alone. Not only was my body being challenged but so was my mind. I was feeling confused, anxious, depressed, and lonely. I felt like I was wavering in all of my commitments, and I didn't want to get out of bed most days. I cried often because I felt weak and defeated, and I knew another surgery could set me back both mentally and physically. I knew exercise was a way to release my frustration and feel in control, so I tried to focus on the goals I had set. I tried to find things that made me feel happy by setting small goals that seemed achievable in shorter amounts of time. When I started going to a gym, my focus was on building up the leg muscles as a short term goal. I started running on their track and setting small goals there too. I even swam in the pool to switch up the routine. I started committing slowly to other things as well. Sometimes in life, we need to enjoy the journey in order to make it to the destination. Had I not set small goals along the way, I might have quit altogether, but because I didn't quit, the journey was more enjoyable, and all the small goals I set, I accomplished.

My morning radio show host friend and encourager arranged for me to be on the radio to discuss my journey and to help inspire others to run their race despite their circumstances. I got to meet the Crim Race organizer, and we were all on the radio together for a fun and inspirational discussion. This amazing experience reminded me to be grateful for the ability to run and participate fully in life, without giving up.

The Friday night before the Crim, I was getting ready to run the Michigan Mile. It's a one-mile race the night before the Crim, and it starts in front of the University of Michigan in Flint. Thousands of people participate in this race because it's a fun race, and there's not a lot of pressure to be a top finisher. I trained for this one-mile race, and I was going to give it my all and finish no matter what. I'm very competitive so finishing in less than eleven minutes was my goal. My husband was by my side, and my friends cheered me on, as they understood the journey I was on. My husband had never run a race before, so I was so happy when he agreed to run this race with me along with my good friend Caroline and her daughter. Like I said before, a mile is a mile no matter how long it takes to get there, so I ran it a quarter-mile at a time. I limped through the running. I was sweating harder than ever, and I mentally coached myself through each quarter-mile. It literally felt like the race was taking forever like I was running in slow motion. But guess what? I ran that mile like my life depended on it. I also did it in ten minutes and thirteen seconds, putting me at fifteen out of fifty-one women in my age group. I ran my race, and I was proud of my results.

I did a lot of soul-searching during the three months before the race. I did hard things that weren't hard for me before the accident. I was challenged in areas that had never been a challenge to me before. But through all of it, I persevered. I never persevered alone, though: I prayed for God to help me through all of it. I had my husband, my family, my friends, doctors, and therapists who helped me and cheered me on through the crazy journey. Without all of them, the race would have been just another race. What I learned is we never persevere alone. All of these people were the added ingredients to my success. God will always be present through the storms, and sometimes, He sends some pretty awesome people to ride through it with you.

What are a few steps you can take when going through a storm of your own?

What small goals can you set for yourself to accomplish living your best life?

Ed, me, Caroline and Eliza
One Mile Race August 2017

Chapter Eleven

"His master commended him: 'Good work!
You did your job well. From now on be my partner.'"
Matthew 25:21, MSG

My Dad

SEPTEMBER-OCTOBER:

On Labor Day weekend, we made last-minute plans to stay in a motel on a lake in my hometown. I wanted to show our foreign exchange student my hometown and introduce him to my family. When we arrived in town, I immediately wanted to go by and visit with my dad. I hadn't visited my dad much that year due to my injury. He was in the late stages of Alzheimer's. They had just bought a new house and downsized so my stepmom could manage it alone, and I wanted to tour it. When we got there, my dad was sitting on the couch watching television. He seemed as though he knew who I was when I sat down next to him, but I think, if anything, maybe he just recognized my voice. I sat next to my dad, not saying much as he dozed in and out of a nap. I tried to engage him in conversation every now and then, just rubbing his arm as he sat and napped. He would wake up occasionally and mumble something to me. I remember telling my dad I loved him while he seemed alert, hoping he would remember me as his daughter and respond back. He just gave me a smile with this half-grin on his face. It was a comforting smile and one of gentleness and love.

My stepmom gave us a tour of the house, the garage, and the backyard. We focused on the beauty of the backyard, its size, and potential for quite a long time. We finally decided we should go check on my dad, and as we approached the garage, my dad was opening the door to look for us. I'll never forget my dad standing there in the doorway looking confused and helpless. It was so hard for me to see my dad in that stage of Alzheimer's. I took his hand and led him to the kitchen to sit down, then I hugged and kissed him goodbye. We left to go back to the motel, as it was late and he had a hard time later in the day.

We continued our weekend fishing, bike-riding, visiting friends and family, and just hanging out. Time always flies when you are having fun. Monday came, and it was time to head home. We stopped by my dad's house for one last goodbye before we left. My dad was in a stage where he slept a lot, so when we stopped, he was sleeping in bed. We visited for a while with my stepmom, hoping he would be up for a visit, but he slept the entire time. I walked by his room to check on him; he was restless but continued to sleep, so we said our goodbyes and went home.

A week later, my dad got sick and ended up in the hospital. He had a bedsore, wouldn't eat, was dehydrated, and was acting really out-of-sorts. My dad was in the hospital for three days before he was admitted into a nursing home for wound care on his bedsore. It was hard for this wound to heal because it was on his lower back side. As weeks went by, we watched my dad suffer in pain from the wound and from Alzheimer's. My dad went from moments where it seemed he remembered me and talked to me normally, to moments where he just stared at me because he was unable to talk anymore. I'll never forget the day tears ran down my dad's face as I looked at him and told him I loved him so much and I wished I could take his pain away. I told him he didn't have to hold on anymore for us; Jesus was waiting to welcome him into Heaven. My dad slept most of the time, but this one particular day, the day before he passed away, he looked me in the eyes and mouthed the words, "I love you," as tears streamed down his cheeks. I pressed my cheek up against his and cried with him, holding his hand. I told him over and over how much I loved him, how sorry I was that he was suffering, and that it was okay to let go, while at the same time, I wanted him here one more day, week, month, and year so I wouldn't have to live without him. I personally had never watched anyone suffer for that long to understand how painful it was to watch someone you love die.

Time was getting shorter with my dad, and everyone knew it. My drive to see my dad was an hour and a half one way, and the next day, I was taking the early shift and my sister Shannon was taking the afternoon shift with him; we were so mentally and physically exhausted from driving, we decided to do shifts so one of us would always be with my dad. My two kids, my granddaughter, and I visited with my dad as they said their goodbyes to him. I thought my granddaughter Bella was going to be scared, but she went right over to her great-grandpa and hugged him, said her goodbyes, and told him how much she loved him. She only had four short years with him, but her love for him was evident. Small children have a special way of just loving without an agenda, and it was so sweet yet so sad to watch. My daughter was almost twenty-five at the time, and she had so many memories with her grandpa that she will always cherish. He had such a special place in his heart for her. She struggled with her goodbye as she hugged and kissed him for the last time. My son, who was a teenager, also said his goodbyes as he hugged his grandpa for the very last time. As my sister Shannon and her boys showed up to take the second shift, we left with heavy hearts, not knowing what tomorrow would bring. The odds were stacked against him, as the staff was sure he didn't have but maybe a day or two left. I left knowing that whatever God's plan was, He always knows best.

The six of us had a small early celebration for Marissa's upcoming twenty-fifth birthday when we arrived home. Bella purchased her mommy presents and really wanted her to have them. We tried to celebrate the best we could even as we all ached at the thought of what was to come. We chose to celebrate, even if it was through sorrow and pain. After a couple of hours, I became overwhelmed with this weird, unsettled feeling. I had not heard from my sister, and I felt compelled to call her. Something didn't feel right. In the same moment I called her, my dad began to pass, as his breathing was changing. My son Dawson and I jumped into the car, and we flew to the nursing home. Thirty minutes into the drive, my sister informed me my dad had passed. I never drove so fast to get anywhere as I did that night. It's almost as if I thought I could stop him from passing if I could get there fast enough. It's funny the things we think we can control that aren't at all possible.

I cried all the way there in disbelief that my father, the man God chose to love me and raise me, was now in Heaven, and I'd no longer have him here to hug me on earth. The day was October 25, 2017. I was angry my dad had suffered so long with Alzheimer's and that it robbed us of so many years together. I was angry that my dad did not get to enjoy retirement the way he should have after so many years of hard work. But, I will never forget the day almost three years prior to his passing when I asked my dad if Jesus Christ was his Lord and Savior. He looked me boldly in the eyes, almost offended I'd asked him the question, and with certainty, he said, "Yes." So, although I might be angry about all the reasons my dad died, I'm also glad I know without a doubt he is in Heaven. This provides me the hope and assurance that one day I will see him again in a place where he will no longer be suffering from Alzheimer's or be in any kind of pain.

Five days later, on October 30, we buried my dad and said our final goodbyes. I knew my dad was in Heaven with Jesus, playing golf, with the most beautiful crown that had been placed on his head, as Jesus said to him, "Well done, my faithful servant, well done."

I wrote this poem for my dad after he died:

Today I said goodbye
I didn't know what else to say
All I did was cry
It was a really hard day.

Dad I really miss you
It's only been five days
Since the day you left us
Every day is grey.

I cry many tears
I want to sleep away my day
I walk around numb
I wanted you to stay.

I know that you were sick
And Alzheimer's took your brain
But it can't steal my memories
because your love heals my pain.

No dad could ever compare
Dad you were the BEST
I hope you love Heaven
Now it's time you rest.

When you faced a difficult situation that was out of your control, how did you handle it?

My Dad

Chapter Twelve

*As bad as you are, you wouldn't think of such a thing.
You're at least decent to your own children. So don't you
think the God who conceived you in love will be even better?*

Matthew 7:11, MSG

The Gift

NOVEMBER:

Two days after I buried my dad, I was having my third surgery to remove all the metal from my leg. I didn't like the limp I had when I ran and the morning pain I felt in my leg, so surgery was my only option to hopefully help with that. Thankfully, the surgery went so well that I never experienced any pain. I did, however, have an annoying hard cast on my leg and had to use the knee cart again, but only for two weeks. To be honest, the two weeks went by pretty quickly, and boy was I glad I didn't need any pain medications at all. It was rather easy compared to the other surgeries I had. After the two weeks were over in the hard cast, I had to wear a walking cast for two weeks. I really didn't feel I needed it for the entire two weeks; walking was much easier this time since the surgery hadn't been as complicated or severe. However, I did abide by the doctor's orders and wore the boot, especially out in public, for safety measures. I still had people driving me places because my leg was weak, but I told my church that I was available and if they needed me to volunteer to help with anything, they just had to let me know when and where.

One day in mid-November, about two weeks after surgery, I got an invitation from someone to come and help decorate the church before Thanksgiving, to get it ready for Christmas. I let them know I'd be glad to do so. During this time frame, God had put it on my heart to forgive the person who crashed into me that day. The only way I could do this was through a letter as a way to show him that I understood it was an accident. I didn't want this person to sit at home and feel bad for what they had done. Although I was unsure of the facts, I was certain it had to have simply been an accident. I picked up the phone and called my lawyer the day I was supposed to decorate. I told her I wanted to write a letter of forgiveness to the man who crashed into me, and I'd like for her to get it to him somehow. She agreed to do it, and we hung up. I then received a phone call from the church letting me know they wanted me to come in to decorate the next day on Friday, November 17, instead of that day. I agreed.

The next day, someone picked me up to go and decorate. I limped around with my boot on helping to hang things and decorate trees. I decided I needed to sit for a little while and help decorate some wreaths, so I sat in the youth action center. Another member of the church joined me. "What happened to your leg?" she asked.

I proceeded to tell her details of the car accident and the most recent surgery to remove the metal from my leg. As we talked, another woman from the church walked in and asked me about my leg. She overheard me say I was in a car accident. "Yes," I told her. "I was in a car accident on my way home from work one day."

"Where did the accident occur?"

"Fenton Road," I replied.

"When did it happen?"

"January 25th," I recalled.

"Do you know the person who hit you?" she asked.

I found it a bit odd she would ask me such a personal detail, but I proceeded to tell her the name.

Her face didn't change at all as she calmly said, "That was my husband."

I, shocked and confused, repeated, "Your husband?"

She said, "Yes. That was my husband who was in that accident."

Immediately, I began to cry. I instantly knew what this meant. She continued to tell me that they never knew anyone was ever hurt, as the insurance company told them nobody was. I sat there in complete shock, and I'm pretty sure my face showed it. I felt a weird hot sensation come over me, almost numb to what I had just heard. We went to the same church and saw each other almost every single Sunday. I had never been asked by anyone outside of my family what the name of the man was. Had one person in the church ever asked me, they would've known right away. This man opened doors for us as we entered the church almost every Sunday; unbeknownst to either of us, we were the people in those cars that day. He opened the doors with a welcoming smile, and I'd smile back as he helped us into the church. His wife said, "I need to go and call my husband and tell him so he can come up here after he's out of work and meet you." She went on to say, "He's never going to believe this."

I could hardly believe it myself. What I did know, and it was very clear to me, was God's timing is always perfect. He knew my heart, and He knew I was ready to receive this gift from Him. I was in the right place to be loving and kind. Just the day before, I was going to write a letter of forgiveness to this man; I spoke it, and I meant it. But God knows us so well. He knew a letter would be so impersonal to me. He knows I'm a relational person, and I would need to do this in person. He set the stage and put us in the same place at the same time, and we were both obedient. We showed up to decorate. Then, in the most intimate of places, His house, the place we both have in common, He showed up with the one thing only He could give me. No human could have given me this gift; it had to come from Him.

While I waited for her husband to arrive, we talked all about that day. I asked her how the accident happened, and understandably, she wanted me to wait and talk with her husband. We continued to decorate the church, and we continued to talk as I cried because it felt so surreal. I felt as though this was a dream. Neither one of us could believe this was happening; I mean, what are the odds? Not a single person who witnessed this miracle take place had any clue what had just happened besides the two of us.

I must say I was a little bit nervous as her husband approached the church. I assured his wife I wasn't angry and I had already forgiven him. When he arrived, we met outside by their vehicle. All he could do was shake his head in disbelief. I hugged him, as he looked very sad. I wanted to reassure him that everything was okay. Although I was walking around with a boot on, it was the last surgery, and I'd be walking around cast-free in no time. I told him how, just the day before, I was going to have a letter of forgiveness sent to him, how I wanted him to know I wasn't angry anymore, and God had answered my prayers. He, unfortunately, wasn't feeling the same way. He felt remorseful and sad he caused me so much pain. He felt bad because he saw me every Sunday as he opened the door for me. However, we all agreed had I found out any sooner, I may not have received it the same. I may have still been so angry inside that I wouldn't have forgiven him, and my heart would not have been right. It could have caused division.

The moment had come when I finally got to ask him the big question, the one I had been wondering about for ten months. I was feeling so sad for him, I almost forgot to ask.

"What happened that day that caused you to drift into my lane?" I asked him.

He replied, "I really don't know, other than everything went black and then I woke up."

He had blacked out and nobody knew why. He felt bad because the insurance company had assured him nobody was hurt. The entire time, he had no idea anyone was suffering. We exchanged phone numbers, and I pleaded with him to go home and not to feel bad at all. I now knew it was truly an accident, and I wasn't angry anymore. His wife gave me a lift home. We agreed to not name anyone when telling the story to people who knew us to protect his privacy. He didn't want anyone to look at him like he was a bad person.

Truly, he is one of the nicest people anyone could ever meet. Every Sunday since, we hug, talk about our jobs and things that are going on with our families. He always asks about my leg and still shakes his head, but he also knows God is so good and I am healed. Not only is it amazing to me that we've all gone to the same church for the past five years, but now I have gained new friends. I have gained a special relationship that may not have happened had I not given it all to God and let Him handle it, had I not lived by faith and realized that the only way I was going to find out was through God's timing. My heavenly Father knew I spoke forgiveness from my heart the day before and blessed me with a gift only He could give me. The timing was so perfect, except now I couldn't share it with my dad.

As I consider the timing of this gift and why it happened when it did, the only thing that made sense to me was that although my earthly father was gone, I now knew how much my Heavenly Father loved me, I am not fatherless, I could turn to Him and ask Him for anything, and He loves me even more than my own earthly father did. I had never experienced a love like I experienced that day. I couldn't tell my husband this story without crying. Everyone I told was in disbelief; they all experienced the same chilled feeling I did that ran down their arms and necks. I knew that where my dad left off, my Heavenly Father stepped in. He not only stepped in, but He showed His love for me in a way that was so tangible.

What is a time in your life when you received a gift that you know came only from God?

Chapter Thirteen

*If any of you lacks wisdom, you should ask God,
who gives generously to all without finding fault,
and it will be given to you.*

James 1:5, NIV

The Second Gift

Two days later, on Sunday, November 19th, we went to church, and I wasn't feeling the greatest. I had a headache, and it just wouldn't go away. I barely made it through the service. After church, we went out to lunch and then went home. The headache got worse, so I decided to lie down and sleep it off. When I have a migraine, I know I need to sleep in a room with no noise or light, so I went to my room and took a nap. During this nap, I had an extraordinary dream. I dreamt about the cover of this book and the title. I actually woke up to me saying the title of the book over and over. My husband came into the room, as he heard me talking and he figured I was awake.

"I heard you talking and was wondering who you were talking to," my husband Ed said to me.

"You'll never believe this, but I just had a dream of a book title and what the cover would look like," I said. "The title is *Broken Redefined*, and I'm not sure what that even means."

I told him I felt it was a vision from God. I was supposed to write a book. I went on to describe the cover as a black background with the title in white chalk writing, a bird's nest, and one whole egg sitting in the nest.

After listening to the details of my vision, he said,

"Looks like you are writing a book then."

God knows I need things to be clear without a doubt that it's coming from Him. About nine months prior to this dream, my friend Caroline gave me a journal and instructed me to write things down because someday I might want to write a book. I laughed and thought this was crazy. She obviously didn't know I had only found an interest in reading books a year or so prior. Besides, who is going to buy a book about a person who broke their leg with nothing significant to go along with it? Nobody cared that I broke my leg. I can tell you right now: nobody, and I mean nobody, could have ever predicted how this story was going to unfold. For the next six months, God confirmed to me over and over what the cover of this book was going to look like. God must have been speaking through Caroline because things happened when I was with her. We went to an antique shop about two weeks later, and there it was, a huge canvas with a bird's nest and eggs in it. I called Caroline over to see it because I knew she wouldn't believe it.

We both looked at each other and laughed, and Caroline said, "Well, looks like you are writing a book," as we agreed that once again God confirmed He wanted me to write this book.

A few weeks after that, I was at a bookstore shopping for a book. It's a huge store, with thousands of books on shelves; a bookworm's dream come true. I walked over to the Christian book section and randomly pulled out a book, and it had a bird's nest on the cover of it with eggs in it to replace the letter "O" in the title. Talk about chills. I couldn't help but silently laugh and shake my head. Yes, I bought that book as a reminder of my assignment from God. That might seem silly to some people, but it seemed fitting to me.

On another occasion, my husband and I went four hours north on a vacation. We went for a stroll and came upon a tiny gift shop, and on our way through it, I looked around and saw at least a hundred tiny bird nests with ceramic blue eggs in them, sitting on shelves, randomly placed around the room. I laughed out loud and pointed them out to my husband who laughed and shook his head.

In the weeks that followed, just about everyone I knew on social media was posting about a bird's nest that was built either on a door hanger, in a nearby tree, or in the framework of their house. It became a daily hobby reading their updates on the changes in the nest and the growth of those bird eggs. Everywhere I went for weeks, I was reminded at least once a day of a bird's nest and a blue egg nestled in it.

Today, as I sit here writing this book, I am reminded that just as those baby birds were growing inside the eggs, I am growing as a writer. Just as a tiny bird has to endure the pains and struggles of hatching, growing, and flying to be a bird, I must go through the struggle of growth to become a writer. I was being reminded daily growth takes time, patience, and nurturing. Without the warm, patient, love from a mama bird, those baby eggs would never grow or survive in the nest alone. Growth happens during the different seasons of life and with the warm, nurturing love of our Father. He can nurture us to become all we are supposed to be during those seasons.

As I'm writing this chapter, I'm about three weeks shy of the first gift God gave to me during my recovery, the gift of new friends. As I reflect back, I realize He gave me several different gifts along the way. He gave me doctors, nurses, therapists, determination, prayer, laughter, tears, hugs, strangers, wisdom, strength, smoothies, reminders of those I love, grace, mercy, healing, opportunity, love, moments, time, and new opportunities.

People ask me all of the time if I'm glad 2017 is over. Not really. Once I moved past the physical pain, it really wasn't the worst year of my life. I really learned a lot that year about forgiveness, loving my neighbors, giving myself some grace, growth, trusting God, and true friendships. I'd give anything to have more time with my dad, have him hug me and tell me he loves me one more time. I learned that God loves me so much, He waited until He knew I was ready to lose my dad before He took him. I know that sounds strange but had I lost him three years before, I wouldn't have been ready. Most importantly, I wouldn't have had a relationship with God first so He could step in where my dad left off.

Sometimes writing this book was painful because of the reminders of those difficult moments, but they are also reminders to me I'm no longer broken: I'm a renewed person with a renewed heart and soul. I'm so much stronger than I even knew I was. I know that being obedient isn't always fun or easy, but I promise you it will be worth it. I'm not sure that I'll ever fully arrive, but I'll definitely put in a good effort.

Sometimes, we just need to be broken so we can become all God wants us to be. My broken may be different than your broken, but broken redefined can be a significant term for you as well. When you allow God to step in and pick up the pieces, He becomes the substance of renewal that helps hold the pieces of you together during times of brokenness. I want to be honest with you, I never really feel like a whole person. I just feel like a stronger person because I know who my substance is and who I can give my burdens to when I can't handle them on my own. I can't speak for anyone other than myself, but I don't think we were ever meant to feel whole. If we did, then we wouldn't have a reason to seek God if we felt fully capable as individuals to handle things on our own all of the time.

God wants us to reach out to him. His strength will strengthen us to face the challenges life throws at us. Naturally, we want to do things on our own to prove our own strength, but perhaps we should consider reaching out for help as a sign of strength, not weakness. I'm so much stronger with God than I am without him. I've had no faith, small mustard seed faith, and I have had big faith. I can tell you faith wins every single time when you put it in the right places. Just know that when your faith feels as small as a mustard seed, God says that is enough.

Whatever season of life you are in, I encourage you to seek God as your substance to hold you together. You are strong because you reach out to Him to be your source of strength.

Chapter Thirteen

Can you reflect back on a time when you knew God was asking you to do something that you didn't want to do?

Marla and I finishing our first marathon (10/2020)

Marla and I after the marathon

Epilogue

The Lord directs the steps of the godly. He delights in every detail of their lives. Though they stumble they will never fall, for the Lord holds them by the hand.

Psalms 37:23-24 NLT

He Set Me Up

The "good news for you" is the message of this book to others who may need it. I'm sure you've heard the Bible referred to as 'The Good News.' Pastors, missionaries, and people who know God, or may not even know God, use that phrase often in reference to the Bible. Do you see how it all had to happen in God's perfect order? Not my perfect order or timing but God's. When I surrendered my life over to God, ordinal perfection took place that week starting with me speaking forgiveness on Thursday, God answering my prayer on Friday, and then He gave me the vision for this book on Sunday.

God does everything with order. He ordered my steps, and everything had to happen in the order it did for me to receive it the way I did. Forgiveness had to be the first thing I did. Forgiveness opened the doors for me to receive everything else He had in store for me. Once I forgave, He then knew my heart was right and I was ready to meet the man from the accident. That's a gift only my heavenly Father could have given me. He knew by giving me that gift that I could now trust Him as my Father. That led to the confirmation of this book, a simple story to help others who may be struggling with something in their lives. In the end, it all glorifies God and how much He really loves all of us. Even when we are unsure of what to do or how to do it, when God calls us, He qualifies us.

I knew nothing about writing a book, but I heard Him say, "Just write the story, and I'll figure out the rest." He did just that. He put the right people in my path who had also written and published a book. When I reached out, I was led to the publishing company that published this book. I had no idea where to start looking, what a publishing company really did, or what the process of writing a book even looked like. But, He did.

I had to develop as a writer along the way and be patient with the process. Let's throw in a normal work-week, a teenager, an exchange student, a new job, new life goals, ministry, grandparenting, being a wife, then COVID-19, and add online classes to my list of things to do, and the list goes on. All of this while writing a book and developing myself in a way I never thought possible. I had to trust God even when I didn't understand what was going on. God did know it would all work out as His perfect plan because, honestly, I didn't really have a plan. After I wrote the first draft of this book, I never thought I'd actually go through with publishing it. I never saw this book leaving my computer until I received a nudge from God that said, "Send a message to your friends who are publishing a book," so I did. I was so afraid of the unknown, the criticism, opinions, rejection, and everything else in between. But then, I thought to myself, if this book helps one person then all the fear, criticism, and worries will be worth it. After all, Jesus did the real suffering on the cross, and He did it for just one person. YOU.

My story was just an ordinary story until God stepped in and turned it into an undeniable love story. Without His presence in my life, this story would not have happened, and if it did, it would have only been about a girl with a broken leg. I AM so much more than a girl who had a broken leg because my God is so much bigger than that. HE defines who I am. I am broken, redefined as transformed, with God as my substance that holds me together.

How have you been broken, redefined as transformed?

How will you let God define you?

About the Author

April Delor

April is a wife to Ed and mom to Marissa and Dawson. Being a mom has been her hardest and most rewarding job title. She loves being a mom more than anything else. Now that she is figuring out how to navigate life as an empty nester, she is pursuing her career as a health and wellness coach and author, very different from her twelve years as a preschool/latchkey teacher. She is looking forward to all of the things God has in store for her future as a coach, author, friend, wife, grandparent, mom, and servant in the field of ministry. She wants to live a life designed around purpose and intentionality in her career and with family and friends.

CPSIA information can be obtained
at www.ICGtesting.com
Printed in the USA
BVHW031809130421
604843BV00008B/453

9 781952 840067